# MYTHICAL CREATURES COLORING BOOK

## Monsters and Beasts from around the World

ILLUSTRATED AND WRITTEN BY KAREN LEONARD
WWW.KAELLYNN.COM

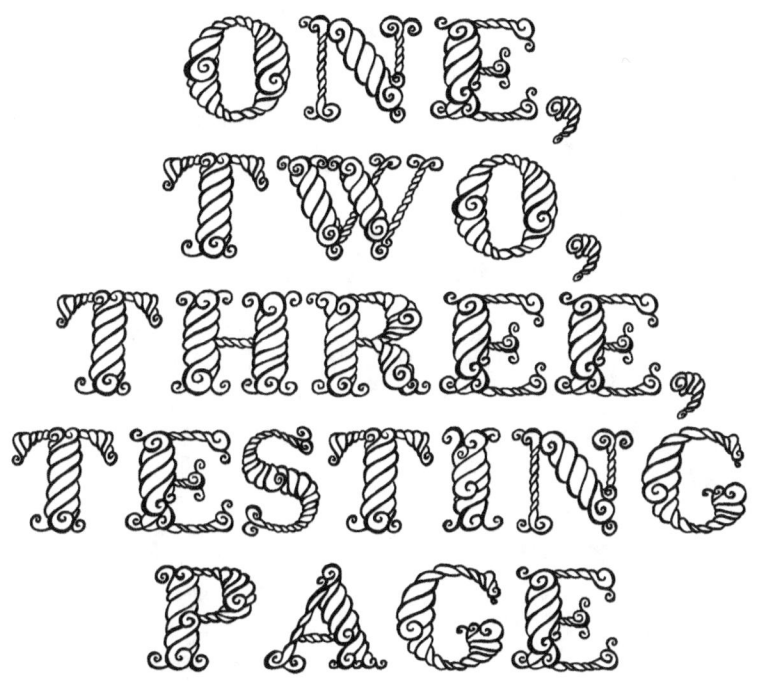

# ONE, TWO, THREE, TESTING PAGE

Use this page to test out your colored pencils, pens, markers, and anything else you would like to use while coloring in these creatures. Many pages in this book are intentionally left blank or are filled with informational text about the mythical beasts, so that ink bleed-through will not affect the other illustrated pages. If you have a heavy-handed approach to coloring, you may wish to place an additional page between illustrations or cut out the pages and complete coloring them on a different surface.

# FOREWORD

Many of the creatures in this book have multiple names, varied origins, and multicultural iterations. The text accompanying each creature is just a snippet of a conversation that I held with them and found particularly interesting.

I chose to seek out and illustrate mythical creatures because they fascinate me. Some of these creatures are scary; they are the monsters that guard dangerous waters and eat naughty children. Others are explanations of the mysterious. What sort of creature could leave bones washed up ashore in such an intriguing formation? And others are divine. They bring rain, protect us from nightmares, and provide blessings to the deserving. My hope is that coloring these creatures will help you find the answers to something mythical in your own life. Enjoy coloring!

This book is dedicated to Kaida Dawn, my little dragon.

# AIRAVATA

I was born from the shell of the Cosmic Egg with my eight elephant brothers and reborn again with my mate from the Cosmic Ocean of Milk. I am the king of all elephants, as pronounced by Brahma himself. My rider is the storm king of the Devas, and he throws his thunderbolts at anyone who dares to disrespect me.

We rode together once against the Cosmic Dragon who greedily stole the waters of the earth and drank its rivers dry. The dragon fought for many days and nights before the storm king slayed him on a mountainside. I healed the earth by reaching down into the wells of the underworld with my trunks and filled the clouds with lifegiving water.

# ARACHNE

SHEARING, CARDING, SPINNING, DYEING, AND WEAVING, I DID IT ALL. I WORKED HARD FOR MANY YEARS TO GROW MY SKILLS AND I BECAME THE BEST IN MY VILLAGE. WHEN I TRAVELED FARTHER, I SAW THE TALENTS OF OTHER WEAVERS, AND THEIR CREATIONS WERE POORLY CONSTRUCTED COMPARED TO MINE. I CONTINUED TO PRACTICE WEAVING, AND MY TAPESTRIES WERE REGARDED AS THE BEST AND MOST BEAUTIFUL IN THE LAND.

BUT EVERYONE INSULTED MY HARD WORK, SAYING THAT I WAS TAUGHT BY THE GODDESS ATHENA! IT MADE ME SO MAD THAT WHEN ATHENA HERSELF CAME TO SEE MY CREATIONS, I CHALLENGED HER TO A CONTEST. I WOVE A PARTICULARLY OFFENSIVE TAPESTRY SHOWING HER THE FALLACIES OF THE GODS. ATHENA WAS AWED BY MY BEAUTIFUL CREATION, BUT SHE COULD NOT LET MY PRIDE GO UNPUNISHED. SHE TRANSFORMED ME INTO A SPIDER, CURSING ME AND MY DESCENDANTS TO WEAVE FOR THE REST OF OUR DAYS.

# ARGUS PANOPTES

I used to be a Giant in service to the goddess Hera. With my one hundred eyes, I could keep watch even throughout the night, as my eyes could sleep in turns. Using my Giant strength and vigilant eyes, I could guard anything.

Once, Hera gave me a white heifer to watch over and told me to tie it to an olive tree. Unbeknownst to me, the heifer was a nymph in disguise that the god Zeus wanted for himself. Zeus sent the messenger god Hermes to charm my eyes asleep. Then Hermes killed me and set Io free. Hera was angered by this, but she knew that I was not at fault: how could a mere Giant hope to stand up to the machinations of the gods? Upon finding my slain body, she transformed my eyes into the feathers of a peacock so I could stay watchful forever.

# BASILISK

FEAR ME, THE KING OF SNAKES! MY EGGS ARE LAID BY OLD COCKS AT MIDNIGHT, AND I HIDE AMONG THE CHICKENS UNTIL I AM STRONG ENOUGH TO KILL. MY EYES CAN KILL WITH A GAZE, MY BITE IS VENOMOUS, AND MY BREATH RELEASES POISONS INTO THE VERY AIR SURROUNDING ME. I HAVE LAID ENTIRE FIELDS BARREN, SPOILING WHEAT PLANTS WITH MY AWESOME PRESENCE.

MANY TRAVELERS THROUGHOUT OUR LANDS CARRY ROOSTERS WITH THEM, KNOWING THAT A ROOSTER'S CROW IS THE SAFEST WAY TO KILL A BASILISK. ONCE, A MAN RIDING ON HORSEBACK HAPPENED UPON ONE OF MY KIND IN HIS PATH. HE USED HIS SPEAR TO KILL THE BASILISK. AS IT DIED ON THE END OF HIS SPEAR, THE BASILISK'S POWERFUL VENOM TRAVELED UP THE WEAPON, KILLING THE MAN AND HIS HORSE.

# BLODEUWEDD

Lleu Llaw Gyffes, a powerful mage who could not be killed in day or night, in or outdoors, while riding or walking, clothed or naked, or by a lawfully created weapon, became cursed to never take a human wife. With the help of other mages, they created me. I was shaped from many flowers and magicked into a maiden to become his wife.

But I did not love him. I found out his secret and arranged to have him killed with a spear crafted unlawfully during masses. The assassination had to be performed at dusk while he wore a net, with one foot set firmly on a cauldron and one on a goat. Despite my careful planning, Lleu escaped at the last minute. They punished me with yet another transformation, changing me into a flower-faced bird: the owl.

# BUNYIP

I HAVE LONG SINCE FORGOTTEN ALL MEMORIES OF MY HUMAN LIFE. I RECALL BEING CURSED INTO THIS FORM FOR EATING SOMETHING PRECIOUS, BUT WHAT IT WAS, I DO NOT REMEMBER. I HOPE IT WAS DELICIOUS.

I IMAGINE SOMETIMES THAT I HAD A FAMILY. A WIFE AND CHILDREN. I SEE WOMEN AND LITTLE ONES APPROACH THE BANKS OF LAKES AND SWAMPS THAT I INHABIT, AND SNAP SNAP CRUNCH, I EAT THEM UP RIGHT QUICK BECAUSE THEY ARE THE MOST TASTY.

I DON'T THINK MANY PEOPLE KNOW WHAT TO WATCH OUT FOR. I HAVE HEARD A LOT OF MY YUMMY DINNERS YELL, "WHAT IS THAT?!"

# CAT SITH

I'm supposed to steal the souls of the dead before their burial, but people entertain us all the time at wakes! They leave out catnip in rooms for us to play with and give us funny riddles to solve. I like curling up near fires and watching them play games. If they do this enough, then I get a little too distracted and then I don't get the chance to walk all over the dead one to take their soul.

Sometimes witches transform into Cat Sith, and we don't mind too much. But they can only change back and forth eight times. On the ninth time, they're stuck! I think being a Cat Sith is better anyhow: all the saucers of milk left out are for us to lick up.

# CATOBLEPAS

I GRAZE ALONE AT THE PURE SPRING AND SOURCE OF THE NILE RIVER. ONLY MY IRON STOMACH CAN WITHSTAND EATING THE ROOTS OF THE POISONOUS PLANTS GROWING HERE. IF I DID NOT EAT THEM, THE POISONS LEECHED INTO THE WATER WOULD DESTROY EVERYTHING ALONG THE NILE.

THE OTHER ANIMALS DO NOT UNDERSTAND THAT I AM PROTECTING THEM FROM THE NOXIOUS PLANTS. THEY APPROACH THE SPRING, BELIEVING ALL THE VEGETATION TO BE SAFE. SO I MUST MAKE THEM AFRAID OF ME BY LIFTING MY HEAVY HEAD AND GAZING UPON THEM WITH MY DEADLY EYES, OR BY RELEASING A CLOUD OF POISONS FROM MY BREATH. THEY MOSTLY AVOID ME NOW. I AM ALONE, BUT WITH PURPOSE, AND I ENJOY THE SOLITUDE. THE NILE IS MY CLOSEST FRIEND.

# CHINTHE

My wife kicked me out. How could she do that to me?! I took my rage out on the people of the land, mauling and terrorizing them. So strong was my fury that no one could defeat me for many years.

My son had my strength, but he did not know me, as I had to leave when he was very young. He tracked me through Burma and we fought. I died that day, but when he found out that I was his true father, he became so grieved that he used my likeness to guard the local pagodas. Now my stone figures guard many pagodas and scare away enemy spirits. When needed, my statues emit frightening roars that can be heard into the heavens.

# DRAGON

Somewhere deep in these mountains is my lair, but it would be quite the foolish human to attempt to find it! I would rend you limb from limb, smash you against the rocks, and toast you in my fiery breath if you tried to steal from me. The gold, jewels, and heaps of precious treasures that lie within are mine, carefully collected over thousands of years for me to curl up around and admire.

Armies cannot stand against my kind. What hope do you have? Leave now, before I decide to make a tasty snack out of you. In fact, all this talking has made me very hungry...

# FENRIR

I will begin Ragnarok, the final destiny of the gods. I will kill the one-eyed god Odin, eat the sun and moon, and devour everything in my path. But that same prophecy also foretells my doom. I am not eager to start Ragnarok if it means my own death. I choose to rest here in the cold snows of the North and hope that those days are still far ahead.

In fact, the gods like playing games with me. I do so love games. They bring chains to see if I can break them, and I snap them easily with my amazing strength. Nothing can hold me, and if they do find something that can bind me, well, perhaps I will not hesitate to begin their final destinies after all.

# GHILLIE DHU

Come young child, do not pout,
You're not lost, I've found you!
These birch trees are my home,
And I can lead you out.

Give me your biggest smile,
Show me those white teeth.
Ew, a few have to go-
Those two are rotting, vile!

Let's tie them to this fence,
And run away quickly!
Then I will send you home
With pockets full of pence.

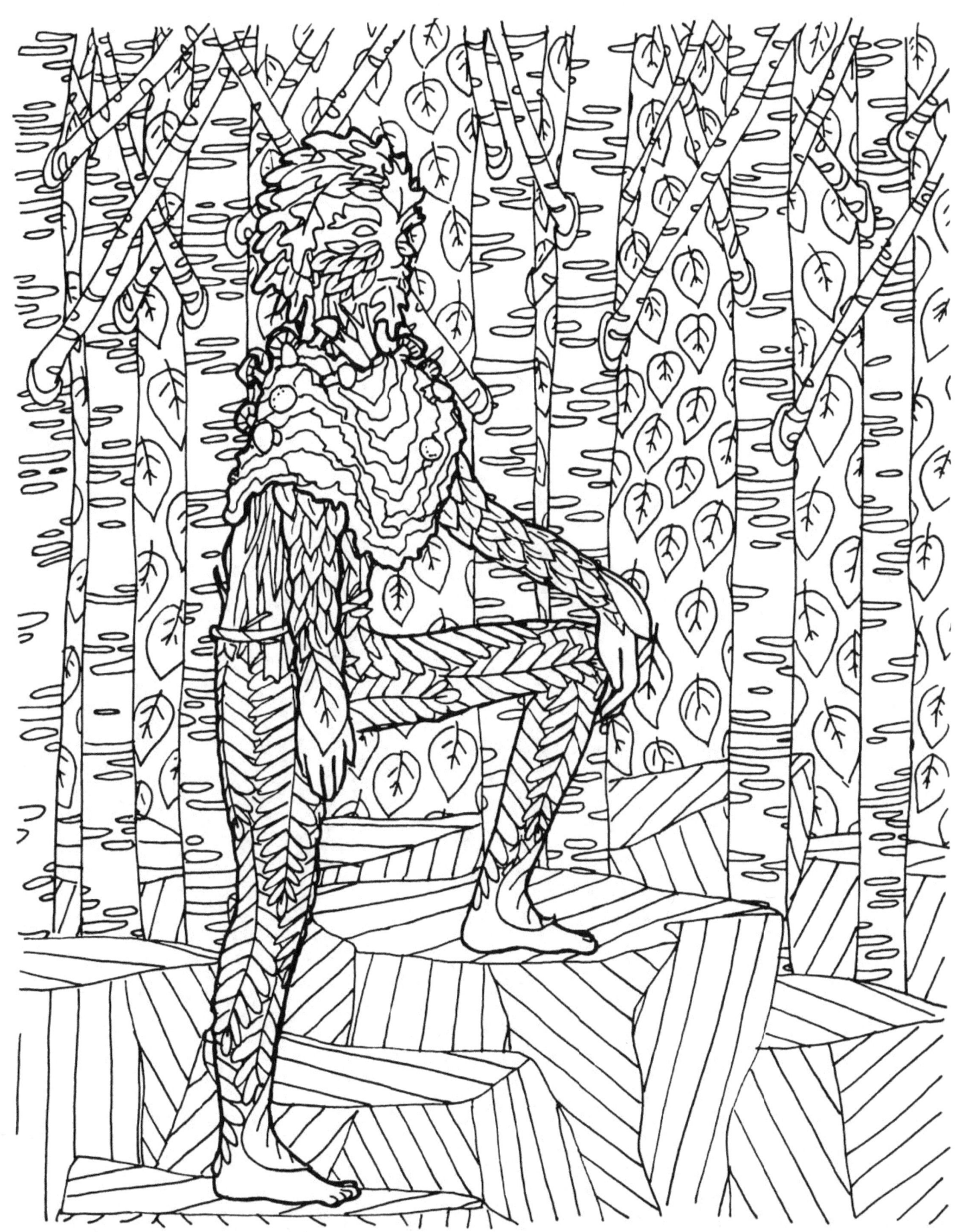

# GOLD-DIGGING ANT

Our hive is large enough to chase away the intruders on camels that would steal the gold that we excavate from the desert sands. Each one of us is bigger than a fox, more vicious than a lion, and faster than a horse. The riders can be clever, they like to arrive when the sun is hottest and we are resting below the surface. If we do not gather quickly, they are already gone with sacks of our gold.

Our queen hates it when we lose gold to the camel-riders. She enjoys gathering it all up in mounds for our little ones to climb and play on. The gold shines brilliantly in the desert sunlight, creating a sparkling display that can be seen for miles.

# GRIFFIN

Griffins are called the kings of all creatures, and my kind are feared for our power. We are solitary, never taking flight with each other. So I never knew what our kind truly looked like until I found a village with Griffin statues over their doors. I visited it every day, looking at these statues like they were mirrors, and I enjoyed viewing them.

The villagers were deeply afraid of me, and many moved away. Those that remained avoided me. One did not run away at the sight of me. I taught him everything I knew, which was quite a lot more than he knew with his limited lifetime. When I finally left the village, taking a few Griffin statues for myself to admire, I threatened everyone with my red-hot tail to treat him well. I've heard that he now has the highest station, the largest home, and the most friends.

# HAKUTAKU

I KNOW YOU. I USE MY EXTRA EYES TO SEE IN DREAMS AND I FIND YOURS SOMETIMES. I FEAST ON YOUR BAD DREAMS, AND I REMEMBER THEM ALL.

THE YELLOW EMPEROR ONCE FOUND ME UPON A MOUTAINTOP. HE WISELY ASKED ME ABOUT ALL OF THE DEMONIC YOKAI SPIRITS PLAGUING HIS LANDS. I WAS ABLE TO REACH INTO THEIR DREAMS AND REVEAL TO THE EMPEROR WHAT THE YOKAI WERE MOST AFRAID OF. HIS ADVISERS TOOK COPIOUS NOTES AND USED MY KNOWLEDGE TO STAVE OFF MANY DISASTERS.

KEEP A PICTURE OF MY LIKENESS NEARBY. THE YOKAI ARE AFRAID OF ME BECAUSE OF WHAT I KNOW FROM THEIR DREAMS. IT WILL MAKE IT EASIER FOR ME TO FIND YOU, TOO. I CAN EAT UP YOUR NIGHTMARES AND YOU WILL SLEEP EASIER WITH ONLY GOOD DREAMS.

# HIPPOCAMPUS

The sea god's chariot is drawn by four Hippocampi. They ride swiftly during the storms at sea and can bring him on land, transforming into horses as needed.

I am not one of Poseidon's noble steeds. A water nymph confronted me in Atlantis and commanded me to find her a handsome man to seduce. I found a strong man who excelled at sports, and she rejected him, saying that he was too short. Then I sought a tall man, who she said was too shy. The next one was too foolhardy, then too stupid, then too vain, and this situation went on for many weeks until I exhausted the supply of men in Atlantis and came to her empty-handed. I stood alone in front of her for judgment, and she accepted my friendship. Now we explore the oceans together.

# HYDRA

The more I am cut down,
The more I grow back.

My blood gives life to me,
Yet poisons all others.

You can find me in a lake,
And the entrance to the Underworld.

I am a serpent,
My brothers, a lion and a dog.

All of us immortal,
Yet all defeated by Heracles.

# JACKALOPE

They're sitting around a campfire and telling ghost stories. Someone has carelessly left out a flask of whiskey, and I steal a few swigs while I listen to their stories. When the embers have almost burned down, I hop behind a log and imitate their drawl.

"Have you heard the one about the Jackalope?" They guffaw, and tell me that no one believes in my kind.

"Well, I heard that the Jackalope can gnaw through the bones of sleeping cowboys with their needle-sharp teeth. And since the teeth are so small, you don't feel a thing. You just wake up with one less leg!" They nervously laugh this time, begin to wonder which of them is telling the story. A few of them do not sleep that night. The joke's on them, though: I only eat plants!

# KAPPA

On my head is a small pool of water, my life-force. Once, I tried to drag a farmer's horse into the nearby river. The farmer ran up and greeted me with a bow. I am no uncouth barbarian! Of course, I bowed in return. But this tilted out my life-force, dripping it all off of my head. I froze in place. How could I function without my source of natural energy?

The farmer rescued his horse while I was incapacitated and put it back to work in the fields. I suppose he took pity on me, because he scooped up some water from the river and filled my pool. Perhaps other kinds of Yokai would be mad with embarrassment, but not us Kappa! We don't hold grudges, and, truthfully, the farmer saved my life. Now I bring him presents of fish from the river, and he keeps a delicious cucumber patch just for me.

# KRAKEN

When I change course, so does the sea. Currents follow me and if I choose to, the swirling of my tentacles can create deep whirlpools.

Some sailors came into my territory purposefully. They wanted to fish on the plentiful crop that always surrounds me. This is how I got entangled in a net once. The net had so badly twisted up my tentacles that I couldn't thrash and cut out of them, but I am so heavy that the sailors couldn't drag their net up. They tried to pull me up for several days before cutting their net loose and sailing away.

Now I strike any ship that dares to come near. I will push my way to the surface, wrap my tentacles around the mast of their ship, and drag the lot of them down into the depths! No one will trap me again.

# LAUMA

From my diamond throne on the moon, I saw a woman below who had trouble with childbirth, so I came down to help her. I gave her hot stones for her aching back and told her of my own journeys through birthing. One month later, she became the mother to a baby boy.

Her family grew larger, and she had to work harder to support them by working in the fields. One day she left her first son behind in the fields when she went home. I watched over him until she returned later that night, worried and frantically searching for her child.

I brought him back to her. "I've seen you work hard for your family, so I have kept him safe for you." I gave her baskets of food and some jewelry from my collection. Her children grew strong and healthy, and she became the grandmother to a happy family.

# MANTICORE

I can mimic your speech, human, but I prefer to sing with my trumpet-like voice. It rings out loudly and brings more of your kind to me. And when they come, I choose the fattest one to eat up!

As a youngling, I escaped a group of hunters that tried to smash my tail. The stingers in my scorpion tail hadn't fully developed yet. If I meet those hunters again, I will be able to let the deadly stings fly like arrows into them, then devour them. I gladly await the day we meet again, for I am strong and they will be feeble compared to my might.

# MBOI TUI

Let me slither among the swamps,
my belly loves the humid wetness.

Let me admire the flowers here,
My eyes prefer these living rainbows.

Let me dance with the others,
My heart grows in kinship with its creatures.

Let me feast on the insects and pests,
My beak crushes them into tasty snacks.

Let me protect the Ibera Marsh,
My piercing squawk warns hunters to run far.

# MERMAID

I was separated from my sisters, and couldn't find the way across a treacherous path. The sea looked different with the changing tide and ships above casting down shadows. I did not know it at the time, but I had gotten caught in a current that brought me to a port.

Even worse, a bad storm washed me up on the shore. A few sailors found me crying of helplessness, and they took pity on me. They rowed me out to a deeper part of the water, where I could not get washed ashore again. Their vessel still travels the seven seas, and I follow them, giving them gifts of pearls when I find pretty ones. I have yet to find my sisters, but at least I have protectors while on my search.

# NINE-TAILED FOX

I can transform into a woman, but I choose not to do that anymore. I fell in love with a man and came to him as a beautiful woman. We had children together, and we were a content family.

One of my children wanted a dog so desperately, but I refused. A dog would find me out! My husband did not know this, and thought I was simply being stubborn. He eventually gave in to our child's wishes and brought home a puppy for her. It barked and sniffed and pawed at me, knowing my true form. I became startled, changing back into a fox. Everyone was so surprised, but I was just embarrassed. I jumped the fence, ran away, and have not gone back to my human family ever since.

# OUROBOROS

I AM BIRTH AND DEATH, THE BEGINNING AND ENDING OF TIME. I AM
THE CYCLE OF REJUVENATION: FROM STRENGTH TO WEAKNESS. FROM MY
FORM HAS SPRUNG THE UNIVERSE, THE SUN, AND THE EARTH.

I AM THE WHEEL AND THE RINGED IRIS IN YOUR LOVER'S EYE. I AM
THE NUMBER OF NONE AND INFINITY. BECAUSE I WILL NEVER END,
NEITHER WILL YOU. WE ARE NOTHING AND EVERYTHING.

# PEGASUS

Bellerophon, the greatest hero of Greece before Heracles, captured me with a golden bridle. At the time, he was on a quest to clear his name of a great wrongdoing. He was charged to defeat the fire-breathing Chimera.

I flew him straight to the Chimera's lair, where Bellerophon cleverly stopped up its fiery throat with an ingot of lead before killing it. Then he was sent on many other quests, which we defeated handily. His exploits made him too proud, and on our journey to the home of the gods themselves, Mount Olympus, he fell and became crippled for the rest of his days.

I do not miss Bellerophon, for now I travel with the god of thunder and carry his bolts.

# PHOENIX

I think the sun is watching me. I like to splash around a well to clean my feathers at dawn, and the sun seems to come up a little bit later each day. She lingers right on the edge of the horizon while the sky grows lighter, until she finally must rise.

She knows I am growing older. Perhaps she is curious to see my own rising. When I die, my body will burn up, feathers and all. The sun's first light at dawn will reignite those flames and I will be reborn in my old ashes as a young phoenix, ready for another thousand year-long lifetime.

# PSYCHAI

Speak my name and I shall come to you, certainly in dreams. You could be lucky enough to enjoy me in the waking world, too. All you have to do is pursue me, and I will follow you anywhere. We could have an adventurous romance, I just need you to leave your cares behind.

Sell everything you own; you will not need those material things. And with your money, you don't need work so hard. We can relax together or run away, just the two of us. Your friends will understand. They will see a man with no worries, and be inspired to pursue their own hedonistic desires, just like we did. Come with me!

# QUESTING BEAST

I am the rejected, monstrous son of a devil and a woman. I found a home in King Pellinore's woods, where the trees are tall enough to conceal my presence. I eat sheep and cows from the local farmers, and when too many go missing, then they search for me. Sometimes his people catch a glimpse of my spotted fur, and I must spend weeks in hiding.

It is easy to hide from the hunting dogs, as my voice bays like a dozen hounds. It is harder to conceal my strange appearance, and King Pellinore has vowed that if he never slays me, then his sons will take up the quest to kill the beast.

# QUETZALCOATL

Up in the sky, you see the fifth sun. When the fourth sun died, darkening the earth, the creatures living on our world perished in the many earthquakes that occurred without its life-giving light. My brothers worked together to build a large fire and sacrificed one of us to give life to the sun. Another jumped in the fire, just behind the first, and his life became the moon.

There were no creatures left on the earth, so I journeyed to the underworld, intending to raise the dead. The lord of the underworld chased me out, but not before I had gathered up a few bones. Once I reached the surface, the earth goddess helped me. She ground up the bones into a fire, I turned it into a paste with my blood, and we shaped the dough into humans.

# SATYR

I'll provide the music if you'll provide the dance. We can drink a bit of wine and enjoy the night together. Don't be shy: there's much more wine in the cellars that I keep hidden and cool. I stomped the grapes myself many seasons ago and it's quite tasty now!

Stay long enough and you may see the Muses. They come to listen to my melodies and eat from my cooking. We have great fun! They put my likeness in the sky. Look up into the night sky and you can find Sagittarius, my stars, with a wreath thrown down at my feet.

# SPHINX

Which creature has one voice, yet becomes four-footed, two-footed, and three-footed?

One sister gives birth to the other, and she, in turn, gives birth to the first. Who are the two sisters?

There is no shame in not knowing the answers. I usually eat up the travelers who do not guess correctly. I'm feeling lenient today. Man crawls on all fours, walks on two legs, then uses a cane in old age. And for the second, the sisters of Day and Night give birth to each other at every dawn and dusk. I think I will not let you pass. For not knowing the answers, you will have to find another path.

# THUNDERBIRD

There is a large mountain fortress floating above the clouds where you cannot see. This is our home, where we Thunderbirds make our nests. We fight among each other for fun and to prove our strengths. When we get too excited our wings flap mightily and create loud bursts of thunder.

We must be careful among the people. Our human sons must not use a bow and arrow. Once released, their arrows will turn to lightning and start storms. I had to pluck my grandson from a forest fire that he began with an arrow and bring him to our mountain. He is safe here, but can never rejoin his family on the surface.

# UNDERWATER PANTHER

At the bottom of our lakes is a treasure trove of shiny raw copper. My children like to play with the golden rocks, using them for their games. The copper is lucky, and we must do what we can to protect it from thievery. We will push boats into the shallow reefs, cutting up their hulls. We will muddy the waters so none can see the glint of metal. When the boats are too large for us, we will call forth storms to sink them.

Canoes that cross the lakes must take a certain path to avoid angering us. Even in winter, we will crack the ice if anyone comes too close to our territories in the lakes.

# UNICORN

I PREFER TO FIND A QUIET PLACE TO DRINK WATER AND NAP ALONGSIDE A FRESH STREAM. WHEN I REST, THE OTHER ANIMALS QUIETLY SLEEP. THE BIRDS CEASE THEIR WHISTLING CHATTER, SQUIRRELS FIND THEIR NESTS, AND FOXES STOP THEIR HUNTS. I CREATE A SMALL BUBBLE OF SERENITY THAT NO ONE BUT THE LION CAN PIERCE.

THE LION VEXES ME! ALL THE CREATURES WAKEN WITH EXCITEMENT TO WATCH US QUARREL. WE CHASE EACH OTHER THROUGH THE LAND WITH OUR NATURAL WEAPONS; HIM WITH HIS FEARSOME TEETH AND CLAWS, ME WITH MY LONG SPEAR-LIKE HORN. I CAN RUN FASTER, BUT HE IS MORE DETERMINED TO SEE ME LEAPING ABOUT AT HIS WHIM.

# WILL-O-THE-WISP

It's so dark out, and you look lost! Do you need help finding the path out of here? Come with me, I can show you a shortcut out of here. I know where all the treasures in these woods are buried. I bet you would like to take a look while you're here. A leprechaun's gold is kept under this tree: I think you should dig it up.

You found some! This must be so exciting for you, now let's get you home safely. Follow me, and we will get through these dense woods quickly. Never mind the sound of water. That's simply an underground spring. Just jump over this small ditch. Don't look so skeptical, for I've already made the jump. See, my light is over here now. A quick step and we're halfway home!

# WORLD TURTLE

I swim through the stars, one of many creatures in the vast sea of the milky way. My shell contains the world, so I must be careful to move slowly or the world would shake. The landmasses on it are so delicate; the wrong shift will cause earthquakes, volcanic eruptions, and landslides. I must rotate around the sun, letting light and dark take to the lands.

Once, my flipper got burned on a hot rock that sped past me. I had to tilt out some of the water on my shell to cool off my poor flipper. The remaining waters flooded the lands and did not settle down for many days. I felt bad, but I need my flipper to keep swimming through the great space that I occupy. I must treat this world with care and show it to all of the stars.

# YATAGARASU

I HAVE BUILT MY NEST ON THE SUN SO I CAN SEE THE LAND CLEARLY LAID OUT BELOW ME. WHEN MY SHARP EYES SPOT A TASTY SNACK, I SWOOP DOWN TO EARTH AND SNATCH IT UP WITH ONE OF MY THREE CLAWS.

I HELPED THE FIRST EMPEROR OF JAPAN DISCOVER AND CONQUER MANY OF HIS ISLANDS. I WOULD SURVEY THE LANDS AHEAD OF HIM FROM THE SUN, THEN FLY DOWN TO PERCH ON HIS STAFF. WITH MY GUIDANCE, HE TOOK HIS FIRST LANDS.

THERE ARE MANY SHRINES TO ME NOW. YOU CAN FIND A PRIEST TO GIVE YOU AN IMAGE OF ME THAT HAS BEEN PURIFIED. IF YOU BURN IT AND EAT THE ASHES, I WILL GUIDE YOU TO SPEAK ONLY THE TRUTH.

# YETI

The locals see me, and they know to keep their distance. They tell their children that I am harmless. This is true. I would not hurt a child, or someone who accidentally crossed my path. But I cannot stand the new tourists with their flashing lights and guns!

Look closely when I whistle. The falling snow will bend around the path of its sound. And I can direct my whistles to a mound of snow on a slope, causing avalanches when I need them. This is for the overly curious creature-hunters that do not leave when I throw rocks at them! People are getting bolder these days. I wish they would find the creatures in their own backyard as fascinating as they do me.

www.ingramcontent.com/pod-product-compliance
Lightning Source LLC
Chambersburg PA
CBHW051944280526
45789CB00009B/3167